How to achieve

100% in a GCSE

A guide to revision and exam technique

Written by a teenager for teenagers

Second edition

Robert Blakey

ISBN 978-1-4452-0277-8

Thanks for the idea Dad!

Preface to the Second Edition

The second edition of 'How to Achieve 100% in a GCSE' has been edited, updated and expanded by Patrick Blakey – the younger brother of the original author Robert.

This edition has been appropriately adapted to suit the newer GCSE courses of the past few years. This has included the removal of coursework (which no longer exists in GCSE), the subsequent addition of controlled assessment (which replaces coursework), the addition of several new revision techniques which were successfully used by Patrick for his exams, and the general proof-reading and editing of all other sections in the book. Patrick has also re-formatted the book to make it an easier, more professional read.

At GCSE level, Patrick achieved 9 A*s – in Biology, Chemistry, Physics, Maths, German, French, ICT, English Lit and English Lang – and 2 As – in Latin and Additional Maths. From September 2012, he is studying Economics, Maths, German and Latin at A-level.

In a similar manner to Robert, Patrick completed the project in his summer holidays after he had taken his GCSE exams. Upon completion, all changes were fully approved by Robert and amended where necessary.

September 2012

Contents

Introduction

Who is this book for?

This book is for anyone who wants to achieve great results through exams and for anyone who wants to fulfil their academic potential. My ambition in writing this book is to help other students succeed in their exams. I want to help 15- and 16-year olds achieve their GCSE goals and to allow them the chance to receive the results that they deserve.

I hope to reveal to you, in a simple way, just how it is possible for everyone and anyone to do extremely well in their GCSEs. I will look at how you achieve top results by focusing on two equally important aspects: revision technique and exam technique. I will show you how - if these principles are applied to every subject - anyone can and will do well at GCSE level.

Who is writing this book?

I (Robert Blakey) am writing this book. I am 16 years of age (at the time of writing), having just finished my GCSE exams. I achieved 10 A*'s, in four of which I gained 100% UMS* (French and the three sciences), and an A in Additional Maths (of which the highest grade you can achieve is an A).

I first came up with this idea – to publish a book about exam preparation – when I found that there was very little information already available on the topic, after much searching around on the internet. If there was any useful advice out there, it was often very limited or difficult to find, yet at the same time, GCSEs are important exams that every teenager in the country has to take. Therefore, I wanted to produce a clear and concise guide on how to make the 'GCSE journey' stress-free, successful and enjoyable (yes - I said enjoyable!). I have done this by bringing together all the experience and useful advice that I've collected over a few years of taking exams into one book.

I decided to write it all down into a book as I enjoy both writing and helping others. At the same time, I am a quiet person, so I felt the best way in which I could help people at this age was by writing about a topic which I felt strongly about and one which was a major part of my life – exams. I also had a long expanse of holiday to do it in (- remember that: you get 3 months of holiday after your GCSEs are over!). Some people may think I'm crazy - writing a book whilst on holiday - but I find this much more worthwhile than having a traditional summer job. So, let's begin as I reveal to you the secrets behind GCSE 'victory'.

* The GCSE marking system, which uses Uniform Mark Scale (UMS)

marks, scales your 'raw mark' up or down depending on the exam's difficulty. Therefore, it is sometimes possible to make a few mistakes but still gain a 100% UMS mark, making the goal to achieve 100% in a GCSE slightly more feasible!

Revision Technique

This is the first element of preparing for any exam, which is certainly very important. Without the knowledge, the exam technique isn't worth anything. This section of the book focuses on the need to make revision efficient and effective and how this can be achieved. When I say 'efficient' and 'effective', I mean that during your revision, you are taking in the most amount of information in the smallest amount of time, and are therefore concentrating very hard.

Revision plan

Before starting any revision, you must make some sort of plan. Please don't ignore this advice because, otherwise, you run the risk of not finishing everything you wanted to do before the exam. A revision plan gives structure to your revision, makes you more organised and in control of your revision. This will make you feel more confident about your 'revision journey'.

However, I understand the point many people make that "You could be spending the time in which you make a plan actually revising". Therefore, don't spend too long on the plan – it only needs to be brief. Being a very organised person, I was in danger of organising my revision too much (for example, writing down exactly which pages of my text book I would revise at exactly what time – a bit OTT!).

So, here's my step-by-step guide to making your revision plan:

1. Get a piece of paper and a pen.
2. Write down all the subjects in which you're going to be taking an exam, leaving space to write underneath each one.
3. Quantify your revision: underneath each subject, write down the quantity of revision required (e.g. the number of pages in the text book or the individual topics that need to be revised).
4. Prioritise your revision: write a number next to each subject from 1 to 10 (if you're doing 10 subjects), indicating which subjects require the most attention in your revision plan (1 = the subject which requires the most revision, normally one of your weaker subjects and 10 = the

subject which requires the least revision, normally one of your stronger subjects).

Once you have done that, it is necessary to decide which type of the following revision plans you are going to use:

- A **time-based** plan: you decide upon the number of hours you will revise each day and estimate the number of hours each subject's revision will take. You then allocate each subject's revision to a time slot in the plan. This is the best plan if you want to guarantee you'll only have to spend 'x hours' a day revising and never any more (or less).

- A **topic-based** plan (this is the one I chose): you decide upon the number of topics you will revise each day (e.g. 3 pages of the Biology text book, one history topic and part 5(i) of the ICT syllabus each day). This is more unpredictable as one day's revision could take much longer than the next day's. However, it's a better way of ensuring you'll fit in everything you want to do before the exam.

Finally, construct and fill in the plan on the computer in a word processor so that it can be easily amended.

Please note, when making your revision plan:

- Vary the revision planned for each day. Don't just do one subject each day. You're much less likely to get bored when revising if you do lots of (smaller) pieces of different subjects' revision each day rather than just one whole subject that day.

- Plan around any events you're going to, during the period over which your revision plan extends across (e.g. if you know you're going to a party all Wednesday afternoon, don't plan much revision for Wednesday).

- Put aside some time to revisit topics that you've already done, to remind yourself of them. For example, if you revise Maths one week, revisit it very briefly the next and then again in a month's time, etc. This will ensure that you don't just forget the revision you've already done, which is especially important if you start revising early on, a long way in advance of the exam.

- Consider unforeseen circumstances. By this, I mean when something happens that affects your revision plan which you didn't previously know about. For example, you get invited out for the day and so have to miss one of your days of planned revision. The revision you thought would only take one day, now needs to be spread over two as it's more work than you previously thought, or new topics arise that you need to revise but had previously not been aware of. Therefore, in your revision plan, always include fairly frequent 'catch-up days', in case you get behind with your revision schedule as highlighted above. One 'catch-up day' for every fortnight of revision would be a good idea. If you dismiss this idea, you'll soon regret it - as I painfully found out, you tend to underestimate (rather than overestimate) the time needed to revise topics.

- Following on from the above point, however long you think the revision of a certain topic or subject will take, add 25% more time capacity into your plan. For example, if you plan to revise quadratic equations, believing it'll take 1hr, allow 1hr 15mins just in case. The reason for this is that it's awful when you have to revise for longer than expected but great when you finish early.

Here are some other important questions many people ask:

When should my revision plan begin from?

Plan to revise from as early as possible. It's never too early to start. After all, the earlier you begin, the more spread out the revision will be and so the less you'll have to do each day. I would definitely recommend beginning your revision from at least the start of the two or three-week Easter holiday, but the earlier the better.

Should I plan when exactly in the day I'll revise?

Not necessarily but I would always suggest revising first thing in the morning onwards, to get it over and done with. Then, you can have the afternoon and evening free and what's more, you're much fresher and more awake in the morning; therefore, you have higher concentration levels.

How much revision should I plan for each day?

I'm afraid it's up to you. The better you want to do in your exams, the more you need to revise. However, overworking and exhausting yourself will not help you in your exams, so there is a limit – it is crucial that you feel you still have enough free time to relax. Becoming stressed and unhappy due to revision won't help you in your exams. I also believe revision is about quality, not quantity. For example, say one person does 6 hours of revision, yet another does just 3. In many cases, 3 hours' productive and efficient revision by a person who knows HOW to revise (perhaps by having read this book!) will do better than the other person who has spent twice as long revising.

How much did you revise?

Many people ask this question. It's very difficult to say because I used a topic-based revision plan (not time-based) and therefore, often varied the amount of time I spent on revision each day. What's more, different people will need to spend different amounts of time revising, depending on their general academic ability and how well they understood the material at school.

Attitude

You can't revise productively without the right attitude to revision. I admit revision is not particularly fun or exciting on its own but you can make it more interesting. I myself don't particularly enjoy revising but nor do I particularly dislike revising. It will not be effective revision, however, if you start revising with a mindset saying, "This is awful. I hate revision". You need to be positive about it.

How can I be positive about revision? Firstly, before you begin to revise, think about all the positives about the revision you're going to do, for example: what are you going to do in your breaks? Which topic do you actually find interesting? Are you looking forward to finding out more about this? How many more marks will you gain in the exam by doing this revision? How are you going to reward yourself at the end?

Secondly, while you're revising, keep up this positive attitude to keep you revising for longer. To prevent boredom, get yourself interested in the subject matter. The GCSE courses were not designed to bore. In fact, the material has all been chosen to interest you, to stimulate your mind and to make you think. Ask yourself questions about what you're learning. Ask yourself what your opinion is on the topic. This is particularly easy to do with subjects like History (with the human context of the subject), English Literature (with all the novels' themes you have to learn about), Religious Education and Science (where you have to look at the 'for' and 'against' arguments of stem cells, for example). For other subjects like Maths, this can't really be done – hence I'm not taking it for A-level because I like to think about the subject which I'm learning!

Also, a good idea is to discuss what you're revising with a friend or parent. Ask them what they know about a topic or what their opinion is. I found this tip especially useful for my English Literature poetry exam, in preparation for which I often talked with my dad about the analysis of the poems I was studying and he was able to offer his interpretation. Revising with others will motivate you and is a lot more fun than doing it on your own.

Finally, if you really do hate every bit of the revision, pretend you don't. Trick your mind into thinking it's great. Say out loud, "I can't wait to revise. I love revising" even if it's not at all true. The root of the problem is that 'revision' has become a negative word; something people constantly associate with negative thoughts or with boredom. This is what you've got to get out of your mind. Your attitude to revision is important. Without the right attitude you won't have the stamina to revise for long before wanting to give up.

The key to be able to revise successfully for longer periods of time is concentration and motivation, both which need to be developed on the run-up to your GCSEs. Firstly, practise concentrating at school. This means not being distracted by your classmates, listening to what the teacher is saying, asking questions, i.e. being involved in the lesson. Take this skill from the classroom back home when revising. Limit the distractions around you and make the revision as varied and interesting as possible - there are many references on how to do this as you read this book.

Secondly, you've got to be motivated to want to revise. Think about why you want to revise? To get great results? Why? Who will you be able to tell about your achievements? How will you feel? Proud? I find revision easier than others because I am self-motivated. However, if you're somebody who doesn't have this character trait, ask others around you to motivate you into revising. Ask your family to support your revision, respect you when you're revising and encourage you to revise, praising you at the end.

In order to encourage self-motivation, set yourself goals before starting any revision. Aim high, but realistically, when setting your GCSE targets. Be specific about your goals – exactly where in that grade band are you aiming? Don't compare yourself to others – everyone should have their own individual ambitions. When you know what results you're aiming for, you should be more motivated into revision. Keep your goals in mind at all times – remind yourself of why you're revising. What's more, you could write them down and share them with someone you respect. In this way, you can check whether your goals are realistic and, once shared, you will be even more committed to their achievement.

Setting

It is essential that you choose an appropriate setting for your revision. I set up a 'revision hub' in my dining room at home. This is because it is away from any distractions, away from the TV, my computer, my Xbox and the rest of the family talking and moving around. What's more, I positioned myself in the room facing away from the window because otherwise, I have a tendency to stare out, watching passers-by! Clearly, if you have a favourite room in the house or one with a better desk, use this as your 'revision hub' – of course, with the dining room being mine, my family had to eat in the kitchen for 3 months!

However, I also noticed that I soon got bored with the dining room. I wanted a change of scenery. This was when I discovered that it's vital to change the environment in which you revise regularly, if at all possible. As well as changing from room to room in the house (but still keeping away from those distractions), you could even move outside of the house.

GCSEs are often taken just as Summer is coming round so, as the temperature and sunshine increases outdoors, so does the temptation to go out – a great idea! If you've got a chair and table or bench outside, off you go and revise under the sun, getting a tan at the same time! Of course, this isn't always practical as I once found out when 30 revision sheets went flying over the neighbour's wall, only for me to hear a sarcastic voice shouting, "Quadratic equations…interesting" – it was my next-door neighbour who was also outside. Seriously though, do try revising in the fresh air because I think it is much more enjoyable than being cooped up in a stuffy room indoors, while the sun is shining outside.

You could even go one step further and revise in your local library or back at school in the library there. This is especially useful, if you're someone who really needs to be physically removed from your home, to not run the risk of being tempted off revision onto the Xbox. I had a friend just like this who decided to revise in the school library everyday during study leave (even though he lived a 45-minute bus ride away!). He said that otherwise he would be too distracted at home and wouldn't end up doing any revision. The added benefit of revising at school is that you have access to your subject teachers, who you can speak to if you need anything explaining. Being a completely new environment, it could make it a more exciting day of revision, too – if you can imagine such a thing!

By now, you will have probably realised one of the key messages of this section of the book – that variety in revision is crucial. You will see this message crop up again and again as we move on through this section as it really is the only way to combat the boredom which so many people find revision creates. The most common complaint I hear is, "Revision's so boring". To that, I say, "Only if you make it so!"

Another idea (which I didn't use) is to devote different rooms to different subjects. This means, for example, you revise all the arts subjects in the dining room but all the scientific ones in the lounge. Although not very practical for many people, it helps you recall the information that you've been revising more easily. It sets the tone for your revision as your mind knows what it's going to revise now and helps to organise all the information in your brain. Then, in the exam, you can picture yourself in the room in which you were revising that subject and recall the correct information more easily. This works because your brain will have associated that room with that subject.

Understanding before revising

The dictionary definition of the verb 'to revise' is 'to review (previously studied materials) in preparation for an examination'. It's about memorising information. However, you will find it more difficult to apply the memorised information in an exam and learn it in the first place, if you haven't yet understood it. Hopefully, you do understand the material from lessons at school and now just need to memorise it. If not, you may need to ask somebody (a parent, friend or teacher) to explain it to you again BEFORE you start revising.

Revision techniques

Once you are sure you understand the information, you need to know how to revise effectively and more importantly, how YOU revise effectively. There is a selection of very different revision techniques to explore. I would give them all a go and see which you prefer. Another idea is to use them all, making your revision methods more varied (this is what I did). The different methods of revising are often suited to different types of learners (kinetic/auditory/visual) – I'll return to this later. Some revision techniques are suited to different subjects - I have mentioned these below each technique. So, here are my different methods of revising, along with my own names for each one!

Visual

For which subjects is this method suitable?

✓ Subjects in which you can easily summarise the information

What do you need?

✓ Coloured pens (gel pens or fine tipped felt tip pens)
✓ A3 plain (not lined) coloured and/or white paper
✓ A creative, artistic mind!

What do you do?

This is the most traditional revision method, tried and tested by generations of students. It is all about summarising (not just copying out) your notes onto paper. You must restrict your notes to just the important facts and those that you find most difficult to remember. It works because this method forces your brain to think about what you're writing down as you summarise the information – that's why it's crucial that you don't just copy it out word-for-word from the text book.

However, try and make this method more fun and exciting by not just limiting it to making lists of notes on lined paper, which is very restrictive and not creative. By making it more interesting and creative, you will stimulate your mind into thinking about the information, helping you to learn it. Also, if the notes look interesting, they will make the subject look interesting.

That is the reason why the colour and large paper are crucial but also, present the information in a variety of different formats – write lists, numbered points, bullet points, text in different colours, different sized text, slanted text or even text going down the side of the page. Even draw pictures and icons which represent different things to you. You could even make a collage, paint or cut & stick – the more exciting you make the page the better - because, if it's attractive and eye-catching enough, it will make you want to refer back to it again afterwards.

You could even use different coloured paper or pens for different subjects; for example, you could always make your Science revision notes on white paper but English ones on yellow paper. This would help organise the masses of information that you're trying to remember in your brain, making it easier to recall the information in the exam. It's similar to the previous idea of revising different types of subjects in different rooms but much more practical.

You must be restrictive about the amount of text you write too – make these notes as brief as possible because that takes less time and forces you to prioritise. This all works very well on mind maps which, when finished, can also be stuck up on your bedroom wall. Then, when you go into your room, for example to get ready for bed, have a glance at the notes up on the wall to remind yourself of what you've been revising recently.

DIY Audio

For which subjects is this method suitable?
- ✓ Subjects in which there is lots of information to learn because this method is quicker
- ✓ Topics which can't easily be summarised, e.g. English Literature quotations
- ✓ Languages (learning presentations and set answers to oral questions)

What do you need?
- ✓ A dictaphone or smartphone with recording software

What do you do?
This is a very different revision method - possibly the least well-known or used. It involves recording your notes out loud onto a dictaphone (a device which records your voice) or onto a smartphone. The notes can then be played back again and again – you can listen to them on long journeys or on your way to school because a dictaphone or smartphone is very portable. The key is to listen to your notes when you are both recording and playing them back on your device.

While this method is much quicker and easier than the previous writing one, it only works if you already have the information you need to revise in a summarised format. This is possible either by transferring your written notes onto the dictaphone or by recording notes from a concise revision guide, being selective (i.e. only recording the important parts).

This method may be particularly beneficial to people who are good actors and so are able to use expression in their voices. When you record your notes, you need to sound interested, using a variety of expression in your voice or else, when you listen back to them, they won't register with your brain. Have fun by experimenting with different voices – there is no reason why revision has to be serious.

Downloaded Audio

For which subjects is this method suitable?
- ✓ Subjects where these recordings are available via the internet or CD
- ✓ Languages

What do you need?
- ✓ A computer with Internet access and/or a CD player

What do you do?
There are several websites online which contain audio recordings of revision notes for specific subjects. Using these notes is a safer option than making your own but they are only available in specific subjects and topics within those subjects. A few of the best that I've come across are:

- *www.bbc.co.uk/schools/gcsebitesize/audio*

- *www.gcsepod.co.uk*

The 'BBC Bitesize' website contains a section full of these recordings which you can either listen to directly on the computer or download onto a mobile or MP3 player to listen to 'on the go'. All the recordings are quite short (a few minutes each) and free.

The 'GCSEPod' website contains more detailed, longer recordings, so is probably better than the BBC's website but you do have to pay for them. Again, they can be listened to on your computer or portable MP3 player/mobile. The recordings are all written by teachers and spoken by actors. There is also a selection of interesting articles on this website about revision and exam technique in general.

For English Literature, there is a selection of very good downloadable audio guides to different novels and plays. To find these, search the internet for '[the title of your novel/play] SmartPass guide'. Generally, these contain a recording of the whole play or novel and the option of having audio notes (about the characters and themes) played to you at intervals in the story. For the additional audio notes you pay a little extra, but they're well worth it.

Then there are language CDs, which are particularly useful for practising listening and speaking skills (which make up about 50% of most GCSE syllabuses). I know 'Lonsdale' and 'CGP' make these – I bought the 'Lonsdale' one for German and French. They're not too long and are a great way of revising for listening and oral exams which can otherwise be difficult to do. Don't say you can't revise for listening exams because you can with these CDs! Play the CD and try to understand the vocabulary as you go along. If you can't, rewind the CD and listen again. If you still can't tell what they're saying, look it up in the accompanying revision guide (which you have to buy separately for 'Lonsdale"s). The 'Lonsdale' CD is also very good for oral practice as it contains all the basic GCSE oral questions, which you can pause, answer yourself and then listen to their perfect answers.

Another useful revision tip specific to a language speaking or listening exam is to simply listen to the audio recording of a past language paper the night/morning before the exam. These recordings can be found on all major exam board websites (OCR, AQA and Edexcel); they help you to get used to listening to the language and get in the French (or whatever language it is that you are taking) 'mood' as I like to say. This is especially effective as a 'last-minute' revision technique to be done just before the actual exam. You can even listen to recordings of past papers that you have already done – simply listening to and taking in the language will help you to prepare for the speaking or listening that you will have to do in the exam.

Kinetic

For which subjects is this method suitable?
- ✓ Any subjects but, in particular, for last minute revision when reviewing visual notes

What do you need?
- ✓ A pair of legs
- ✓ Lots of empty space to walk around in (e.g. an empty house or garden)

What do you do?
It is very difficult for kinetic learners at school as this way of learning is

rarely used. However, luckily, it can be freely used at home. First off, forget the chair and desk, it' time to move!

Place your visual notes or revision guide on a table and read the notes or text out loud. Whenever you come across a particularly important or difficult bit, shout the sentence aloud and use expression to emphasise the key words. In the process, keep moving: walk around the room, jump up and down, go for a run, etc. Try and repeat the sentence without looking at your notes or even act out what you're trying to remember. The more stupid or funnier you look the better!

Video

For which subjects is this method suitable?
- ✓ Subjects for which video clips are available via the internet, TV, CD or DVD

What do you need?
- ✓ Internet access
- ✓ A TV recorder and DVD player

What do you do?
I believe that watching videos is the best way to revise, but unfortunately it is least available in today's market. However, there are some ways to revise by watching subject-related videos and this is probably the most enjoyable revision method for many.

Firstly, keep an eye on *www.bbc.co.uk/programmes/b0080k0c*, where TV programmes dedicated to revising certain subjects are featured. When you get onto this website, click through to 'Episodes' and then 'Available on BBC iPlayer'. There you will find a list of revision videos that have recently been broadcast on TV. You can also find these revision videos on your TV guide and record them for later viewing. They are often broadcast in the middle of the night on BBC 2 during the run up to the summer GCSE period. They are very good and available in a wide range of subjects. There are also some very useful BBC educational revision clips that can be found online at *www.bbc.co.uk/learningzone/clips*.

Secondly, you can look up and rent/buy many other educational videos or even films that have a connection to the topic you're studying - especially in History. All those videos you've watched in lessons at school should be available to buy or rent – ask your teachers for help in finding them. In English Literature, for example, you can always watch the film adaptation (if there is one!) of the novel or play that you're studying, which will always help.

Thirdly, there are many educational computer games and CDs, which sometimes come included with a revision guide. If you like computer games, try these out because you may find them more enjoyable than traditional methods of revising. We tend to associate computer games with fun, which helps to make this revision seem less daunting. The games or CDs normally contain video clips, notes and tests to track your progress.

Test Yourself

For which subjects is this method suitable?

✓ Any but, in particular, for last minute revision

✓ Maths

What do you need?

✓ A parent, friend or covering piece of paper

What do you do?

This is not a revision method to be used to start with. Firstly, another method, such as 'Visual', needs to be used unless you think you already know this subject well enough. This supplementary revision method is about confirming that you have taken the information in, that your revision has worked and finding out how much more you may need to do. It also refreshes your mind on the subject and boosts your confidence before an exam, whilst showing yourself that you really do 'know your stuff'.

You can make this technique more enjoyable by asking somebody else (a parent or friend) to make up questions from the visual notes that you've created or from your revision guide. Hopefully, you then respond with the correct answers! Alternatively, you could cover up the revision guide/visual notes with a piece of paper and shout out loud the answers, if nobody is available or prepared to help you in the house. This is very similar to the way in which you may have learnt spellings in Primary School with 'Look, Cover, Write, Check'.

Friends

For which subjects is this method suitable?

✓ Any for which you know a friend doing the same subject, and preferably the same exam board, as you

What do you need?

✓ Friends who are keen to do well in their exams, like you!

What do you do?

Many of the above revision methods can be done with friends, making them more enjoyable and different as you can discuss the topic you're revising together and then have a chat in your breaks and at the end. However, it is important you don't get side-tracked into talking about last night's football game, rather than the revision! It adds variety to your revision: revise alone and with others.

You can either follow one of the previous revision methods (e.g. audio notes where you record a discussion about the topic between the two of you) or you can just have a conversation about a topic, jotting down any important points that arise in the discussion. This helps the two of you to get interested in the topic as you discuss different viewpoints on, for example, an historical event or a scientific theory. You can ask each other your own personal opinions on the topic – this only works for certain subjects and topics as the previous examples indicate. Also, if one of you doesn't understand something, the other can try to explain it.

Online

For which subjects is this method suitable?

✓ Subjects in which suitable websites are available

What do you need?

✓ Internet access

What do you do?

There are many websites online which will help you revise certain subjects. Obviously, the 'BBC GCSE Bitesize' website contains revision notes (visual, audio and video) along with tests at the end of each topic, helpful to ensure you have successfully understood and memorised the necessary information. You can process the written notes found on these websites in order to create your own notes (using one of the previous methods). Use these websites as different sources for your revision material. The 'BBC GCSE Bitesize' website also has a facility which allows you to draw your own mind maps on the computer – simply go to *www.bbc.co.uk/schools/gcsebitesize/maps*.

There are other general GCSE revision websites containing yet more revision notes as well as subject specific websites containing revision notes (e.g. *www.teach-ict.com* containing games, test & notes for ICT). You can find these using any internet search engine (type in 'GCSE revision notes'). You may have used some of these educational websites during lessons at school which often means your school has paid a fee to have access to this website. Ask your teacher if you're allowed to have the access details for home use, too. The computer can be associated with fun in our minds, so it can seem a more enjoyable form of revision as well as adding variety. However, don't just read these online notes; process them into your own creation to ensure this is an effective revision method, e.g. by creating a colourful mind map from them.

Revision Cards

For which subjects is this method suitable?

✓ Subjects in which there is a lot of simple fact-learning, rather than understanding difficult concepts, e.g. ICT, History

What do you need?

✓ A set of index cards or special revision cards (i.e. small double-sided blank cards)

What do you do?

This revision method combines two previous ones: 'Visual' and 'Test Yourself'. Firstly, you take a card and write down a question on the front, e.g. 'When did the Vietnam War end?' and on the back you can write the answer, e.g. '1973'. Again, similar to visual notes, it is still important to use colour and creativity in creating these card notes, as they are basically a different form of visual notes.

However, the great thing about these card notes is that they can easily be used to test your knowledge on the subject/topic (another revision method previously mentioned). You look at the question, answer it (in your head) and turn over to see if you got it right. Any that you get wrong, you put in a separate pile, which you have to re-test yourself on at the end.

What's more, you could create a game out of these cards to play with others (as I've already mentioned, revising with friends can be a more enjoyable but still effective way of revising). For example, you could use these cards in a game of snap or pairs. For these two games, you would have to create one set of cards with just the questions on and another containing the relevant answers. The games would involve matching the answers to the questions and shouting 'Snap' or 'Pair' at a correct match.

Teach

For which subjects is this method suitable?

✓ Any - but especially ones in which a lot of explanation of your understanding is required

What do you need?

✓ A sibling, friend or parent

What do you do?

The 'Teach' method is a very effective revision technique as it requires you to have understood a topic so much so that you can easily explain it to others.

Essentially, this method is about playing the role of a teacher with a sibling, friend or parent. Simply revise a topic and then attempt to explain what you have learnt to someone else without using a revision guide or textbook – just like your teacher would (I hope!).

You can make this method even more fun by testing your 'student' on the topic after you've taught it. This would work especially well with a friend doing the same subject as you could take turns at being the 'student' and the 'teacher' and test each other in between. Also - if you've got a mini whiteboard, you could use that to draw diagrams and write down key words during your explanation.

This is an excellent revision method in two ways: firstly, it ensures that you fully understand what you have revised and secondly, the act of re-explaining and repeating a topic to someone else helps you greatly to memorise it.

Never Just Read Your Revision Guide!

Many of you may simply read your revision guide or text book. However, in my opinion, this is the most ineffective revision method and is an unproductive use of revision time. The problem with this method is that you're not processing the information, meaning that it's difficult to concentrate and take the information in. It will take you much longer to successfully revise the same quantity of information this way compared to all the other techniques described earlier.

Which revision techniques did I use?

Although I was previously a huge fan of 'DIY Audio', which I used extensively to revise for my GCSE 'mocks', I mostly used 'Visual' for the main GCSE exams. I don't know why - maybe I got bored with using audio notes and wanted a change. I also used 'Revision Cards' for my mock ICT exam.

Then, closer to the exams, I reviewed my visual notes using the 'Kinetic' technique. I often did this outside - weather permitting! I occasionally used the 'Friends' method (helping each other with Physics) and 'Test Yourself' (getting my parents to test me). I also used 'Downloaded Audio' for my language listening exams and 'Teach' on the days running up to all exams. In summary, I used a wide variety of techniques in order to sustain my interest!

Breaks

Before you begin revising, you should be prepared to take a break or even a few breaks during your revision. There is no set time in which you should revise before taking a break, nor is there a set duration for which breaks should last. It all depends on you and your concentration span.

Some people can revise for a long time without feeling the need to take a break and then, when they do take a break, they only take 5-10minutes for a drink. It also depends on the intensity of the revision. If I'm trying to memorise lots of vocabulary for a language exam, I require more frequent, longer breaks, compared to something which I find much easier, such as re-reading my English Literature text. I take a break whenever I feel I need one, whenever I feel my brain needs a rest.

It is important to take breaks as often as you feel is necessary. Whenever you feel like you can no longer concentrate or the information isn't going into your brain properly, take a break. The only exception is for people who like to aim for a time at which they can stop revising, i.e. if you like to work to a deadline. Then, you may consider setting pre-planned times at which you'll take a break, which could feature in your revision plan. I would especially recommend using a pre-planned times system for your revision if you are the sort of person who will easily be distracted or think 'That's enough for today' when you've only done 5 minutes. Pre-planned timing is a disciplined way of revising and should prevent you from rushing your revision just so you can take a break.

It is also worth considering what you will do in your breaks. How will you ensure that when you re-enter your 'revision-hub', you will feel refreshed, recharged and ready to work again? How do you 'recharge your batteries'? Firstly, have a drink in your breaks, preferably water or squash, to rehydrate your body so your brain can perform well in the next round of revision. Secondly, consider exercising during your revision breaks, even if it's just for a short time, e.g. a 10 minute bike ride. Then you will definitely feel refreshed and ready to study again.

Something else which I often did was to revise before I got dressed in the morning, even sitting up in bed if it was practical. I would then take a break in which I would get showered and dressed which certainly refreshed me ready for my next round of revision. This may seem a bit far-fetched but even the fact that you're revising in a different environment (your bed) may help add variety to your revision, reducing the risk of boredom.

The reason breaks are so important is because, as you revise, your concentration levels gradually decrease, so need to be boosted. Without a break, the material you're revising will gradually be 'soaked up by your brain' less and less successfully, taking you longer to properly memorise something, reducing the efficiency of the revision. Therefore, remember: the time taken out in a break will be regained later through more efficient revision, saving you time in the long term.

Rewards

A good way of motivating yourself to revise is to plan a reward for yourself at the end of your revision. This way you can look forward to the end of your revision. The reward could be anything you particularly enjoy doing: Football with your mates or eating a large bar of chocolate! You could even write your reward for each day on your revision plan!

Which source of revision material should you use?

I'm sure many of you have lots of sources of the information that you need to revise. For example, your school notes in your exercise books, text books, revision guides, etc. However, you have a choice of which you use to get the information from. I would personally recommend using a special revision guide rather than a text book or exercise book. This is because it has been specially designed to give you the exact information that you need. It is often only limited to the specific factual information you need to know for the exam, whereas your exercise or text book may contain unnecessary background or detail. Although people have different preferences, my preferred are the 'CGP' revision guides because of their colourful presentation and simple, often silly and funny explanations. Revision guides can be bought from all major books stores, if not already provided by your school and are available for most GCSE subjects.

However, don't totally exclude using your exercise or text books. If you don't understand a topic in the revision guide, want to clarify a point it makes or want to know more detail on the topic, then do refer to a text- or exercise book.

Another useful source of revision material is the official specification or syllabus published for that subject. These can be found online on the examination boards' websites (ask your teacher to find out which board you'll be taking your exam with). Some specifications actually give you the specific factual content of the subject, making it a very useful source of revision material. Others just state what you need to know about but are still useful - you can look up each point on the syllabus, revise it and then tick it off, moving onto the next one, i.e. it acts as a revision topic checklist.

The reason I strongly advise using these specifications is because they have been created by the people who set the exams and are referred to by the examiners in order to create new exams. They are therefore accurate and specific. Often, people ask how much detail they need to know on the topic – these specifications should help you answer this question. Also, they ensure that you're not revising material that you don't need to know, therefore, increasing the efficiency of your revision, giving you more free time.

'Mocks' – they don't matter, do they?

Actually, I believe mock exams are important and you should definitely revise hard for them. The reason is simple – it will help you a lot when it comes to the real GCSEs.

Firstly, revising properly for 'mocks' allows you to figure out which revision technique works best for you by giving you the chance to try them all out. It also gives you practice at using these revision techniques so that you, for yourself, can see that they do work, how they work and which are the most appropriate for certain subjects. Therefore, when you arrive at the time when you're beginning to revise for your real GCSEs, you'll be fully prepared to apply the revision procedure with ease and confidence.

Secondly, think about your GCSE 'mocks'. These are normally taken around Christmas. If you revise thoroughly for these exams, it will cut down on the amount of revision that you'll need to do for the real GCSEs - you'll already be fairly confident with the material when you get to this stage. When you revise for your real GCSEs, the information will come back to you more easily. After all, because the GCSE course is normally two years long, you will have probably forgotten a lot of the material from two years ago if you don't remind yourself of it for your 'mocks'.

Which revision method will suit you best?

The best way to find out which revision method suits you best is to use less important exams like 'mocks' to try out the different revision methods and see which is the most effective for different subjects. Generally, the revision method that suits you best will depend on what type of learner you are.

There are many different types of learner but in general, they can be grouped into three categories: Visual, Auditory and Kinetic. Although one person may learn effectively using a combination of revision methods, I believe you should focus on the revision methods that suit your learning style.

You can use many online tests which claim to show how you learn best. On the following page is my equivalent, but shorter, test, similar to the online ones, which you may want to try. For each row of the table, circle which option you prefer (or write down on a separate piece of paper the number of the column in which your chosen answer features).

1	2	3
In class, I prefer…		
Watching videos	Listening to the teacher	Doing experiments
In my house, I prefer…		
Watching TV	Listening to the radio	Cooking
Outside, I prefer…		
Reading a book/magazine	Talking to friends/family	Playing sport
When I go out, I prefer…		
Going to the cinema	Going to a restaurant	Going to the gym
As extra-curricular activities, I prefer…		
Book clubs	Debating clubs	Drama clubs
I prefer saying…		
"That looks right"	"That sounds right"	"That feels right"

Look at your answers and read the relevant section below:

Your answers are mostly from column 1:

You are a visual learner, meaning you like to learn by reading or watching. The revision methods that'll suit you best are: 'Visual', 'Revision Cards', 'Video', 'Test Yourself' (with 'Look, Cover, Write, Check') and 'Online'.

Your answers are mostly from column 2:

You are an auditory learner, meaning you like to learn by listening. The revision methods that'll suit you best are: 'DIY Audio', 'Downloaded Audio', 'Friends', 'Test Yourself' (with another person testing you) and 'Video'.

Your answers are mostly from column 3:

You are a kinetic learner, meaning you like to learn by being practical and moving around. The revision methods that'll suit you best are: 'Kinetic', 'Revision Cards' and 'Teach'.

Your answers are mostly from a combination of two or even all three columns:

You are a combination of learner types. If you have two columns that feature more frequently in your answers than the other, see the two relevant column number sections above and follow the advice under both. If all three columns feature as frequently as each other in your answers, you like to learn by reading/watching (visual), listening (auditory) and being practical/moving (kinetic). Therefore, all of the revision methods should suit you well!

The ideal world of revision

In an ideal world, you would revise everything thoroughly just once – for your 'mocks' – and then from your 'mocks' until the real exams you'd just keep yourself up-to-date with the information, going over your notes now and again, therefore never actually forgetting it. In the long term, this would increase the efficiency of your revision, reducing the overall time you spend revising. This is what I would recommend doing – it's what I would have done if I could 'rewind the clock' myself.

Little-But-Often Approach

If you're reading this book before or towards the start of your GCSE course, you are at a great advantage and I would strongly recommend you use what I call the 'Little-But-Often' approach. Essentially, this approach would require you to digest your revision into small pieces over a long period of time. For example, if your language course requires you to learn a long list of vocabulary before the exam, if you start early enough (it would have to be at least 6-months in advance) you could probably quite easily learn all the words by doing, say, just 10 minutes of learning each day. This method can apply to many different subjects. In the short-term this revise-as-you-go-along approach would be difficult and challenging but very beneficial in the long-term as you wouldn't have to cram a lot of revision in at the end of your GCSE course.

Summary

The five most important tips from this chapter are:

- Plan your revision **realistically**

- Find your **motivation**

- Discover your **learning style**

- Always revise with the **specification** at hand

- Remember **'Variety is the spice of life'** – and of revision

- Take advantage of the **revision resources** available to you

If you follow this advice, you will be well on your way to achieving 100% in a GCSE!

Exam Technique

Obviously, the most important part of any GCSE course is the exam. It is normally the greatest contributor of marks to the end result and consequent grade. Therefore, the exam is the key area in which you need to achieve. Clearly, doing lots of revision in the ways outlined in the previous chapter helps a lot. However, these days, exam technique is becoming increasingly important too, and hence I've devoted a whole chapter to it.

There's lots of debate out there about whether or not GCSE exams are too easy. Here's my take on this. Yes - the exams may be 'easier' as the media puts it. However, I believe that while they are becoming 'easier' in terms of the factual information which the student needs to know, the types of questions themselves are becoming increasingly difficult.

Exams are moving away from being factual tests, towards having "thinking questions" and "misleading questions" in them. I give the name "thinking questions" to the increasing number of GCSE exams that require you to not just regurgitate facts but to apply those facts in unknown situations, hence making you think – in science, these are the 'How Science Works' questions which I'm sure your teacher will have talked to you about. These questions mean it is no longer good enough just to 'know it all'. It helps if you're naturally intelligent – which you can do little about because your genes control this (so blame your parents!). However, having the correct exam technique, which you can improve upon, is a big factor.

I give the name "misleading questions" to the questions which many different people may interpret in many different ways, hence producing lots of different answers to one simple question. However, the mark scheme with which the examiner has to mark your paper is often restricted only to certain points which count as acceptable answers and others which will not. The problem is that as exams contain fewer factual questions, they contain more and more of these "misleading questions" which can often double up as "thinking questions", too.

Personally, I find some of these types of questions difficult. I'd prefer simple factual questions because I always revise the material thoroughly and it annoys me when I've spent lots of time learning something difficult, yet it then doesn't feature in the exam. One example I encountered during my GCSE exams was revising ray diagrams for mirrors and lenses in Physics. I not only revised this myself but also helped a friend understand how to construct them. Then, in the Physics exam, there were no questions on this large part of the syllabus which I could have answered confidently. Instead, the paper was filled with 'How Science Works' "thinking questions".

Anyway, rather than having a moan about their existence, we need to accept that they're there and learn how to get around them. Here are my tips for dealing with these difficult types of questions.

"Thinking questions"

For these questions, the problem comes down to having the natural ability to think logically and laterally (i.e. 'outside the box'). These questions are easy to spot – any which force you to stop and think before answering – and also make up the majority of GCSE exam questions.

In History exams, all source-based questions are naturally "thinking questions" because you have to apply your own knowledge to interpret an unseen cartoon / poster / article / letter etc. In English Language exams, the comprehension, review / analyse /comment question, inform / describe / explain question, etc. are all examples of "thinking questions" – you're not just regurgitating facts. In Science, 'How Science Works' questions are "thinking questions" – as are the more challenging questions at the end of a Maths exam. You have to apply your own knowledge in new and different contexts.

How do you deal with these questions? You have to ask yourself, "What topic is this question talking about? What do I know about this topic? Does any of my own knowledge on this topic help me understand and answer this question? In conjunction with my own knowledge, what would common sense tell me the answer is?" Use logic and think laterally (i.e. 'outside the box').

Let's test my strategy out. Here's a typical Maths "thinking question", taken from an Edexcel past paper (though all the exam boards have very similar syllabuses for Maths, so this question should apply to whatever board you're taking the exam with). Have a go at this question - ask yourself the questions above if you get stuck.

ABCD is a parallelogram

AB=12cm

BC=8cm

The perpendicular distance of the line DC from the line AB is 7cm.

Area of the parallelogram=84cm²

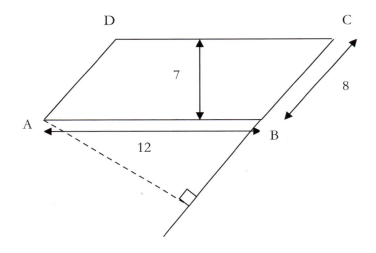

Work out the perpendicular distance of the line AD from the line BC (the dashed one).

Here's how I'd apply my strategy to work out this question (only look at this once you've tried yourself):

1) "What topic is this question talking about?" "This question is talking about the features of this special shape - a parallelogram."

2) "What do I know about this topic?" "I know that a parallelogram: has four sides, has two pairs of parallel sides, which are equal in length to each other, has opposite angles equal to each other and has an area equal to its base times its height."

3) "Does any of my own knowledge on this topic help me understand and answer this question?" "Possibly my knowledge that the area of a parallelogram is its base times height could be helpful because the question specifically tells us what the area of the shape is."

4) "In conjunction with my own knowledge, what would common sense tell me the answer is?" "I know that 7 x 12 = 84 but this isn't the only base and height of the shape that we could use to calculate its area. If I physically turn the exam paper clockwise so that line BC lies horizontally flat, I can see that we could call line BC the base and the dashed line the height of the shape. Therefore, 'line BC' x 'dashed line' = 'area of the shape', so 8 x 'dashed line' = 84, so the dashed line has a length of 10.5cm – the correct answer."

Did you manage to get the correct answer straight away? If so, you're just clever at Maths! Did you get the answer after having asked yourself the questions? If so, this strategy is working well for you. If not, did you follow the strategy of asking yourself each of these questions in turn, to come up with the answer to this typical "thinking question"? Next time you come up against one of these "thinking questions", in whatever subject, try and apply the same principles – the more you practise them, the easier you'll find using them to successfully find the correct answer. When the real GCSE exams arrive, you'll be ready to succeed at what are often the hardest questions on the paper, showing yourself as a very able candidate.

"Misleading questions"

For these questions, the problem is how do you interpret them? Firstly, you've got to be able to spot this type of question. Here are their characteristics:

- They appear complicated

- They may require you to read them twice

- They give you information, e.g. an extract, which you have to read carefully before answering

- They don't require direct use of your own knowledge

- They make you unsure as to whether you've answered them correctly

Here's an example which I fell for. It's part of an AQA Biology Unit 2 question but the information given is not expected to be known at all – have a go at it even if you aren't studying the topic:

Bile is produced in the liver, stored in the gall bladder, then released into the small intestine. Bile contains bile pigments and cholesterol. If the diet contains too much cholesterol, some of it may form 'gallstones' in the bile. These gallstones may prevent bile from moving out of the gall bladder into the small intestine. Bilirubin is a yellow-brown bile pigment. This pigment is produced by the liver from haemoglobin released by broken-down red blood cells.

Suggest how gallstones may produce the following symptoms:

Jaundice (a yellow tinge to the skin).

....

....

....

....

(2 marks)

This question appears complicated, required me to read it twice, gives information which you have to read carefully before answering, requires little direct use of own knowledge and made me unsure as to whether I'd answered it correctly. Therefore, it is certainly a "misleading question".

I struggled to answer this question. I stopped, thought and realised I had no direct knowledge on the topic. Then, I desperately tried to think up some complicated explanation to the question. What's more, it was worth 2 marks (not 1) and gave 4 lines to write on, reinforcing my thought that there must be some special difficult explanation that I had to come up with. This is what I guessed: "As the gallstones block the bile from moving into the small intestine, more and more red blood cells are broken down by the liver, so more and more Bilrubin is released from their haemoglobin. This stains the skin yellow." When writing it down, I knew the answer didn't properly explain itself and showed a clear lack of understanding. It was worth zero marks.

I was shocked when I read the real answer on the mark scheme. Even though the question was worth 2 marks and 4 lines of writing, the correct answer only required three words. The answer "Bilirubin in skin" gets full marks, according to the mark scheme. I had interpreted the question wrongly, wasting time and losing marks.

How had I misinterpreted the question? I assumed that the real answer was a statement of the obvious and so completely overcomplicated the question. Therefore, when I went into any of my Science GCSE exams from then onwards and came across one of these "misleading questions", I asked myself, "What is the simplest answer to this question? State the obvious."

How did you get on answering the question (or was it CBA?). You may have answered the question 100% correctly, writing the same answer as the mark scheme. If so, you don't need to worry about the advice here. However, you may have either answered the question wrongly (like me) or got the correct answer but the long way round, i.e. by writing lots of unnecessary information and at the same time, wasting valuable time. If so, read my advice carefully because every second and mark in an exam is valuable. For you, the problem might be that some questions have become too easy, tempting you to overcomplicate or doubt your answers.

"Factual questions"

A lot of people prefer this type of question, especially if they always do sufficient revision before an exam. However, these straightforward questions are featuring less and less in GCSE exams as time goes by, hence the media may claim GCSEs are becoming 'easier' as there are fewer facts to know. Normally, they make up a minority of the different question types found in one exam paper.

Some subjects are tested more factually than others. Here are some examples. Maths contains a lot of factual questions where, if you have the knowledge, you're definitely going to do well, e.g. solve the equation: $4x + 3 = 10$. On the other hand, some History or English exams often contain no factual questions. In between, Science exams normally contain a mixture of different question types, including some factual questions.

It is very clear how these questions are to be answered – there is no strategy required. The answers to these questions are often just a regurgitation of the facts. They tend to be the questions which require one-word answers (e.g. At what voltage is mains voltage? 230V), multiple-choice questions or fill-in-the-gaps questions. Occasionally, they require longer answers such as 'What is teleworking?' – an ICT question which requires an answer of a sentence or two but is still very factual, as you're just regurgitating a definition.

Reading questions

Before I say anything more, I want you to try this: read this part of a Biology question (similar to one of my previous examples) as quickly as you can.

Bile is produced in the liver, stored in the gall bladder, then released into the small intestine. Bile contains bile pigments and cholesterol. If the diet contains too much cholesterol, some of it may form 'gallstones' in the bile. These gallstones may prevent bile from moving out of the gall bladder into the small intestine. This can cause the symptom of having very pale faeces because a yellow-brown bile pigment (called Bilirubin) will not reach the digested food in the small intestine.

Did you misread the word 'faeces' as 'faces'? Maybe not but I did when I faced a very similar question to this on a Biology past paper. The point is that misreading questions in exam papers is a very common mistake – I'm sure you can remember a time when you've done it before – but should be so easy to avoid doing. Misreading the question is an easy way to lose marks unnecessarily.

There are different ways of misreading a question. You could misread a particular word/diagram/chart/number, such as the example above, skip out an important word (or even a whole sentence) but more commonly, you could wrongly understand what the question is asking you to do.

We firstly need to think about why people misread questions. The answer is based around exam pressure. Some people suffer from this more than others depending on:

- How nervous you are about an exam
- How much the exam means to you
- Whether the exam starts well
- Whether the exam is tight on time
- Whether you have the ability to stay calm under pressure

The greater the pressure, the more you are likely to misread a question, because you panic. This causes you to read the questions too quickly. Misreading the question most commonly occurs towards the end of exams or on longer questions. Towards the end of exams, time pressure increases and concentration levels decrease as you become tired. On longer questions, for example where you have to read an extract before writing, you read the question quickly because you feel like you need to start writing as soon as possible.

Here is a real example of the above (and I'm not just making it up). When I had my real GCSE English Literature exam, I was nervous about it because it did mean a lot to me (I wanted to do it at A-level) and as with most essay-based exams, it was tight on time. It was the exam in which I felt the greatest amount of pressure. I misread the last question ($1\frac{3}{4}$hr into the $2\frac{1}{2}$hr exam) which was also a long one. I didn't read the last sentence of the question, possibly because I'd done several past papers with much of the same format and because I was desperate to start writing.

The sentence I didn't read was there to remind you to write about which poem you preferred and why – something which you had to include in a sentence or two at the end of your answer and something which I had always remembered to include in practice questions. However, exam pressure meant that this time, I not only forgot to include it but I didn't read the helpful reminder to include it. It probably lost me a couple of marks – you might think that's nothing but it is when you're aiming for 100% in a GCSE! If not, it could be the decider between you getting one grade or the other and it's such an easily-avoidable loss of marks – that's what's frustrating.

So, the question is, how do you reduce the risk of misreading a question in your GCSEs? Firstly, if you're susceptible to doing this, i.e. you've made many mistakes in the past due to misreading the questions, think about the possibility of reading every question twice. Although it takes a little extra time, it eliminates any chance of you misreading a question again and so will save you marks. I decided to do this for my Maths exams where I found this had been a common mistake. If this is the same with you, decide to read the questions twice in the exams for that subject, like I did – and it worked.

Another technique to prevent misreading a question is to tick each line of a question as you read it. This is quicker than reading a question twice and encourages you to read it carefully and with focus. By ticking each line, you are confirming to yourself that you have read the line successfully. Whilst this technique may seem tedious and time-consuming, it is so easy to 'skim read' an exam question and interpret its meaning incorrectly.

Often students misread questions because of pressure or lack of time. In this case, try to calm down, relax and therefore slow down your natural reading pace. This can be done by reducing exam pressure - more on how to do this later. Read the ENTIRE question and read it all carefully and slowly, concentrating on every word. In your mind, imagine you're speaking the question out loud, emphasising the key words. Never just assume that you know what it's going to say because you think it's a standard question layout which you've seen many times before. Don't move on from one part of the question until you've fully understood what it's saying. Don't be scared to read it twice. I often had to do this in order to fully understand the information that it was giving me.

The questions for which this advice is most important are those that provide you with information before actually asking the question: English comprehensions, Science extracts, History sources, Maths diagrams, French reading exams, etc. These are where there is the most reading to be done. However, I would also strongly recommend you to read the actual questions before reading the text. This way, you can read the text, specifically looking out for information that will help you answer the questions. At the same time, you should underline any information which you think is particularly important, cutting out any unnecessary background information. This should save you valuable time as you won't have to then re-read the text in order to locate the answer.

Misreading a question can also be avoided by careful checking during any spare time you have at the end of an exam – more on this later.

It is a common but wrong belief that, in exams, you must spend as much of the time as possible writing. Reading is as important as writing. If you don't read the question correctly, there is no way you'll answer the question correctly. As they say, 'the answer is in the question' and that's absolutely true.

ATQ

The most common mistake at GCSE is simply not answering the question. It seems so obvious and straightforward, yet it's surprisingly easy not to 'ATQ' (Answer The Question). This involves either not answering the question at all (by having misread or misinterpreted the question) or, more commonly, by starting to answer the question but soon losing focus, forgetting the original question.

This often happens when the answer required is a long one. For example, English or History essays where one thought might follow another without staying on track with the initial question. Sometimes, people write anything and everything that they know about a topic, as soon as they recognise a word in the question title.

You must ensure that you realise what you're supposed to be answering and clearly show this to the examiner. In order to achieve this, you need to use 'RTQ' throughout your answer (Refer back to The Question). At regular intervals, ask yourself "Am I still answering the original question?" and check that you are by re-reading the question. Highlight or underline the key words of the question when you first see it, so that you can keep reminding yourself of these as you write.

Show, and be proud of the fact, that you haven't fallen for the most common GCSE mistake: waffling on about something indirectly related to the actual question being asked. In your answer, keep mentioning the words of the original question, in order to round off a point and move onto the next. For example, consider the question, "Why did the USA get involved in the Vietnam War?" At the end of one reason, you could conclude the paragraph with the sentence, "Therefore, *the USA got involved in Vietnam* because…" – the words in italics are the exact words of the question. This clearly shows to the examiner that you've kept your focus on the question throughout the essay.

Exam pressure

Many of the mistakes made in exams are due to the fact that the candidate knows that they're being tested and are under pressure to do well from themselves, their teachers and parents. Exam pressure is further increased when the exam being taken makes up the majority of the marks of the full GCSE in that subject.

Therefore, you are likely to feel less exam pressure when taking several modules, rather than just one exam or when the controlled assessment element of the GCSE makes up a large proportion of the marks, as is in languages, for example. Also, taking several modules at different stages over the two-year GCSE period, rather than just one end-of-year exam, can reduce exam pressure. This is because you haven't got the pressure of many exams all together, i.e. the pressure is not as concentrated. Therefore, if you're yet to choose your GCSE options and know you are affected by exam pressure, consider choosing the subjects which are tested mainly by modules and controlled assessment.

Of course, if you're unfortunately much closer to the real exams, here's my advice for reducing exam pressure. If you're under a lot of exam pressure, you'll be feeling nervous just before the exam. Firstly, remember that this is natural – you should feel nervous to an extent – and in small doses, exam pressure ensures that you are motivated for the exam and concentrating hard.

Remember though, that too much pressure can cause you to panic in the exam, so it is important to remain as relaxed and calm as possible in the run-up to (and during) the exam. Before the exam, ask yourself, "What's the worse that could happen?" and then ask yourself, "And what would be even worse than this?" Keep asking yourself this second question until you realise that, "Yes, this exam is important but it's not THAT important." Similarly, if exam pressure is being created by others, e.g. parents, friends or teachers, recognise that they are trying to help but ask yourself the question, "Given that I know myself best, is this advice appropriate for me or not?"

Make sure you do all exam preparation well in advance, leaving you enough time to relax the night before the exam. Doing too much revision the night before an exam will certainly increase exam pressure. Any revision that you do carry out the night before an exam should be 'review-style' revision done in small quantities i.e. going through your notes and recapping what you've already revised. Always leave at least one hour before you go to bed the night before an exam, to relax and take your mind off it. For example, you could watch the TV or even take a bath to reduce your stress levels. And obviously be careful about what time you go to sleep – I'm sure you wouldn't want to turn up to an exam tired or even with a hangover! Also, don't go to bed thinking about the exam but about something you enjoy doing or you are looking forward to - what will you be doing once all the exams are over? This will ensure that exam pressure does not interfere with a good night's sleep – important to ensure you are well rested for the following day's hard work.

Next thing you know, you arrive outside the exam hall and everybody is talking about the exam, testing each other and cramming in last minute revision. Don't bother! Last minute revision is likely to increase exam pressure with negative consequences which outweigh any extra facts that you might pick up. What's more, if you've done the appropriate revision beforehand, there should be no need for you to do any last minute revision. At this point, I would advise not thinking about the coming exam, for, if you do find out something that you've forgotten, it'll only send you into a panic – not a good way to start an exam.

Trust yourself and be confident. I try to do enough revision so that I'll rarely get a question wrong because I don't have the required knowledge, i.e. I believe most mistakes that I make will be for reasons out of my control e.g. a new topic features that wasn't clear in the syllabus, I misread a question or a "thinking question" or "misleading question" catches me out.

When you enter the exam hall, breathe deeply. There is a fine line between nerves and excitement. Try to transfer your fear of failure into the excitement of the possibility of success. When you go to take your seat, smile! Look around and you'll see some glum, unhappy, distressed faces. Do you want to start your exam in a negative frame of mind? Think of the time when you got your best result in an exam. Remember how this felt. Feel happy – you're about to reveal to the examiner all your hard work and fantastic talent for this subject – and you're about to get one more exam out the way, too!

Put yourself in the examiner's shoes

At the end of the day, it is the examiners and markers who matter. They're the ones who set the papers and then mark the papers. These two things will obviously determine your result. So, imagine that you were a marker. Think about what would please you in an exam script. Think about the quantity of papers that you'd have to mark. Naturally, markers are bound to compare scripts with others they've seen before. That means it's important that you make your script stand out from the crowd (in a positive way that is – please don't decide to write nothing just so that you'll stand out!). You've got to prove to the marker, who doesn't know you at all, that you are worth a fantastic mark.

Remember that the markers are always trying to award marks, not take them away. They will read your exam script, looking positively for what you've done well, not what you've done poorly. Examiners will also set the exams in the same way, setting questions that will allow students to show off their knowledge. They do not design the papers to trick you or catch you out – that's not their job.

Time pressure

A lot of people feel that they don't perform as well in exams as they do in classwork or homework. The simple reason for this is that all exams are timed – you have to finish within a specific time. Compare this to homework, where you can spend as little or as much time as you want working on your answer – there is no time pressure. The skill of managing the available time in exams is very important if you want to achieve a top mark at GCSE. It is also important not to let the time pressure add to the exam pressure as this could cause you to rush through the exam.

Obviously the time allocated to a particular exam is the recommended time in which the examiner believes a successful answer can be written. However, I still find that for some subjects I can have plenty of spare time at the end, whereas in others I find myself rushing at the end to finish.

Firstly, it is very important that you follow any guidelines given to you on how long the examiner advises you to spend on each section of the paper, including any reading which has to be done. These time guidelines are normally closely linked to the number of marks each question is worth. If these time guidelines are not present, it may still be possible to see how long you should spend on each question. The more marks a question is worth, the longer you should spend on it. Sometimes, the number of marks available will actually equal the number of minutes of time available, e.g. 45 marks awarded for a 45 minute exam, meaning you should spend no more than a minute per mark.

Secondly, never spend too much time on a question. If you find yourself spending much more time on this question than the last one which was worth the same number of marks, you do need to move on quickly. Leave it and return to it at the end of the exam when you know that you can afford to spend the time on it. The same is true for a question on which you have spent more than 10%-20% above the recommended time guidelines. I know that it is difficult to leave a question because you've got more to write, or think you've nearly got the answer. However, if you don't, you may not finish the paper and will be unable to answer what could be an easier question at the end of the exam. Don't miss the easy marks because you spent too much time trying to get the hard ones. If you are playing 'catch up' because you are behind on time, you might also rush the later questions, whatever their difficulty.

If you find yourself spending too much time on a question, it may mean that you have misread the question or are giving more detail than is required, which won't earn you any extra marks. The amount of marks available should indicate to you the length and depth of the answer which is required. For non-essay based subjects, the number of marks available normally relates directly to the number of points that you need to make in your answer. While it is always a good idea to write down as many points as you can, you must also ensure that you don't waste precious time doing so. For example, I would recommend writing down 2 or if possible, 3 points (but no more) for a 2 mark question. Writing the 3rd point is a good idea as this point acts as a 'safety net' (a back-up in case one of your other points isn't good enough), but writing a 4th point could be using up time you simply can't afford.

Thirdly, you shouldn't finish an exam too early. If you finish an exam very early, this could mean that you haven't answered the questions in enough depth and length, have rushed an answer, have misread a question or even missed one out. However, it is natural to find that you have some extra time at the end of some exams. If so, use it wisely. Never sit with a closed paper in front of you and relax, confidently thinking you've finished. Why not? Because it is impossible to finish an exam paper – there is always more to do.

You must properly check the paper again and again, right up to the time you hear, "Can you put your pens down please". It is tiring and meticulous checking exam papers and that's why some people don't bother. In a way, it can be harder than actually doing the paper in the first place because it's boring. However, it is rewarding when you discover a mistake and correct it, knowing you have just picked up an extra mark.

What's more, you must check your work PROPERLY; otherwise, it is again a waste of time. Read the questions and your answer carefully and slowly. If you just 'skim-read' them, you are unlikely to pick up any mistakes because you're reading it quicker than you did before. Don't assume you won't have made a mistake on 'question x' because you thought it was so easy. Just one extra mark could move you up a grade boundary, meaning you get into your first choice university rather than your second (that's if you're planning on going to university!). One mark can make a big difference.

On the subject of checking your work, here's a technique which I always use which helps ensure that the time you spend checking is most worthwhile. As I go through any exam paper, I always know that there are certain questions which I'm more confident about than others. Therefore, I use a system which helps me to quickly detect the questions which are in most need of checking. I do this because often I will not have enough time to check ALL the questions, just some of them.

Questions which I'm very confident about, I leave blank. Any questions which I'm slightly unsure about, I mark with a dot – this also includes questions in which it might be easy to make a 'silly mistake'. Any questions which I'm very unsure about or haven't been able to complete (due to lack of time or brain power), I mark with a dash. Then, at the end of the exam, I flick through the paper, firstly checking those questions with a dash next to them, then those with a dot next to them and, finally, those with nothing next to them. This ensures that I can easily and quickly locate the most troublesome questions and tackle them in order of priority at the end of the exam when the time pressure is greatest.

Time in any exam is so valuable. You must take advantage of every second you are given – it makes no sense not to. Never lose concentration in the exam. Stay focused, looking down at the exam paper, not smiling at your friend at the other side of the hall or daydreaming about what to do tomorrow. The thing which frustrates me the most is when I glance up from my paper to see my neighbour sat, head on the table, paper closed – there is just no logic in doing so, no matter how confident or clever you are, no matter how much revision you've done.

Practising exam technique

The best way of improving your exam technique is by doing practice exam questions from text books, revision guides, 'BBC Bitesize' (and other similar websites) or, best of all, real past papers. Using practice exam questions, you can apply the advice in this section, so that you are able to use it naturally and confidently in the real exam. What's more, doing this practice is also an effective way of revising in itself – see 'Test Yourself' within the 'Revision Techniques' section.

Past exam papers are especially useful as they allow you to get used to the specific style, timing and format of the exam that you'll take. By style, I mean the types of questions that your exam board tends to use. By timing, I mean the amount of time pressure that you will feel in that exam. By format, I mean the number of questions you must answer, in which order and their suggested lengths – this mostly concerns essay-based subjects. You are likely to do some of these past papers at school but there are often too many to cover, so you can also download them from the relevant exam board's website to try at home.

However, be realistic about how many practice papers you are able to do within the time available before the real exam. You should not rely solely on these papers for actual revision, even though you may find this one of the more enjoyable revision methods. You may want to just flick through some past papers, only having a go at the more difficult questions, skipping out the easier "factual questions" which simply rely on you having done your revision.

Before doing a past paper, think about what exam technique you are going to try out in it – by this, I mean any of the advice found in this section, e.g. "I'm going to read every question twice". Then, when you finish, evaluate the exam technique, e.g. "Did it work? Did I still misread some questions? Is this exam too tight on time to read the questions twice?"

After having completed the past paper, you need to mark your questions using the official mark scheme, which can also be found on the relevant exam board's website. You will then be able to evaluate several other things:

- How was the timing of the exam?
- How are you going to work the timing of the exam better in the next paper you do?
- Which topics are you stronger at?
- Which are you weaker at?
- Which topics require more revision?
- Have you improved from the last paper you did?
- Which type of question most commonly featured in the exam?
- How did you find each question type?
- What can you learn from the mark scheme?
- What must you include in your answer to get a top mark?
- Does the mark scheme include a variety of possible answers for each question, or is it very restrictive?
- What colour socks were you wearing? Are they your lucky ones? – Only joking!

What's more, take a look at some of the exam reports which can also be found on the relevant exam board's website. These reports contain the thoughts of the examiners on each and every past paper and make specific comments on the individual questions – their difficulty, what candidates struggled with, what they excelled at and the common mistakes or misinterpretations made. They also include the grade boundaries for past papers.

They are interesting to read in order to find out more about what the examiners want to see in exam scripts and what they don't want to see. Again, they help you to put yourself in the examiner's shoes (see the previous section on this). There is a lot to be learnt from these reports, especially if you look at those that refer directly to a past paper that you've already done. A lot of the advice given is repeated year after year. Being realistic, I would advise reading one per subject unless you find a particularly troublesome past paper or question and want to read more about it.

Try to remember what you learn from every past paper you do, whether that's from the paper itself, the mark scheme or an exam report. After having done a past paper, take a separate piece of paper and write down anything that you've learnt – anything from exam technique to facts that you weren't aware of before. Then, you can refer to this nearer the time of the real exam to remind yourself of the things you do well (and should continue to do) and the things you shouldn't do or didn't know before. This way, you will successfully apply what you've learnt from this practice to the real exam.

Evaluation is a very important part of doing past papers. Without it, you will learn nothing from doing them, making the process worthless and a waste of time.

The basics

Last but not least, here's a recap of the basics of successful exam technique. Although these may seem obvious to many of you, it is surprising how many people fail to address these simple rules.

Firstly, always read the front of the exam paper, even if you've done so before on practice past papers. It often contains useful information which tells you which questions you should answer, where and how. Although you may know all this beforehand, these instructions can act as a helpful reminder, especially if you're under exam pressure and need some reassurance. The point is that you'll be given time to read the instructions, so why not use that time to do so? Secondly, if there was no point to the instructions on the front, why would the examiners include them?

This leads on to my next point on answering the questions. Make sure you answer only the questions you're supposed to. Also, make sure you write your answers in the correct places on the paper or in the correct individual answer booklets. Check to see if there are any questions on the back page and whether you've accidentally missed out a double page spread (which my friend did, claiming the two pages were slightly stuck together – do we believe him?!) So why does this point follow on from my previous one? Because these specific instructions on how, where and which questions you should answer are clearly given on the front of the paper and so, if read, should prevent you from making any of these mistakes.

Next, expect to sometimes have to stop and think in exams. You're not going to be able to answer every question within a second of reading it. You need to realise this so that you don't panic if you do have to stop writing and think. This is perfectly natural and necessary, especially with "thinking questions" and "misleading questions" (as mentioned earlier). You will only write a clear, flowing and correct answer if you have thought about it beforehand. Examiners want to see that you've thought about your answer before writing it and it's very clear when somebody hasn't – you end up with an illogical, confusing mess!

Finally, if you feel you don't know the answer to a question, don't just leave it blank. There should be no blank spaces in your exam script because you can always do some intelligent guessing. By this, I mean coming up with some sort of possibly correct answer or half-answer, which may still earn you some of the available marks. If you have thought up several possible answers, try and limit the options to a minimum. If you're not confident as to which is more likely to be correct, write them all down, as long as they don't contradict each other. If one of the answers given is correct, you should get the marks. Write the obvious points that come to your mind – anything, no matter how obvious it seems, just guess. You'll be surprised how simple and straightforward some correct answers can be.

Summary

The five most important tips from this chapter are:

- **Practise** dealing with the different question types
- ATQ - **'The answer is in the question'**
- Be aware of the unexpected dangers of **exam pressure**
- Implement a **'checking system'**
- **Relax**, slow down and breathe!

If you follow this advice, you will be well on your way to achieving 100% in a GCSE!

Subject-By-Subject Advice

In the previous two chapters, we have looked at using exam technique and revision in order to maximise your results in any general exam. In this section, we will look at more specific advice for individual subjects, both for the revision of that subject and for applying that knowledge successfully in the exam.

Obviously, I can only talk about the subjects that I've taken, so not all will be included, but often some of the advice I give for one subject will also apply to another. Therefore, I would advise reading all the subjects' sections, even if you're not studying them, because some of the advice is transferable.

Revising Maths

To start off, make sure you have a good textbook or revision guide to work from. Thick, chunky textbooks are good at explaining things in detail but not great for revising with. Therefore, I would recommend buying the revision guide specific to your exam board and specification (if there is one). Otherwise, CGP offer a great range of GCSE Maths revision guides that are very easy to work from.

To begin revising Maths, I would recommend creating some notes on the topics you aren't yet confident enough with. Identify which these are by taking out your text book or revision guide and turning to the contents page. Here, go through all the listed topics, marking those which you wouldn't be able to do if you were given a question now. Don't mark those that you need just a little more practice on (I'll come to these later).

Now it's time to create some notes on these topics. I wouldn't recommend using the 'DIY Audio' revision method because Maths often uses a lot of diagrams, numbers (surprisingly!) and formulae which can only be clearly explained by visual notes. Write down the step-by-step method of answering a typical question from that topic and then give an example. Use your text book or revision guide to do so.

However, it is also very important that you use the 'Test Yourself' revision technique in Maths. Practise what you've learnt because knowing how to solve a quadratic equation and being able to solve a quadratic equation are two very different things. Test yourself by doing practice questions from past papers (particularly the last ones on the paper, which are harder), your text book and revision guide. Include your workings and check your answers are correct. Any topics which you feel you just need a little more practice on, go to the relevant section of your text book or revision guide and randomly pick out a question or two (preferably the harder ones) to improve your confidence with that topic.

As usual, whenever you make a mistake in this practice, highlight it and keep the paper for future reference just before the exam – this includes 'silly mistakes', too. The visual notes you create can also be used for future reference just before the exam, in order to remind yourself of these more difficult topics. Use the 'Kinetic' technique as you review these visual notes and mistakes.

Maths exam

This is the exam in which I find it easiest to make 'silly mistakes', therefore, I always read the questions twice and immediately check my mental arithmetic. It is very easy to rush through simple calculations in your head and get the wrong answer. I also find that this is an exam where I always have plenty of time at the end, so take advantage of this. I check all the questions, including those really easy ones because those are where you're most likely to have made those 'silly mistakes'.

Don't depend on or expect to use your calculator all the time in the calculator paper. For a lot of the questions, it may not be necessary to use it, or it will slow you down if you use it for simple calculations. I once found myself typing '5+7' in a calculator on one of these papers and then thought, "What on earth are you doing?!"

Don't rely on only certain topics coming up in the calculator paper as they can easily put non-calculator topics in this exam, too. In the non-calculator paper, it is easier (but still not safe) to assume which topics won't appear. In a non-calculator paper, I had a question involving pi – something you may not expect without a calculator to hand – but the question asked for an answer in terms of pi, i.e. a calculator question cleverly slotted into a non-calculator paper.

Remember the units – they're not always given for you and will lose you a mark if you forget them. When you come to write your answer to a question, always look back at the actual question to see what you need to convert the 'numbers' to i.e. which units need to be used and whether a certain number of decimal places or significant figures is specified. Sometimes, even if you don't know the answer to a question, if you write down the units of the answer, you'll get one mark!

Show your workings. Even if you get the final answer wrong due to a 'silly mistake', you could still earn plenty of marks through your correct method, if clearly shown. This is most important for Maths where marks are specifically awarded, as shown by the mark scheme, to each stage required in getting the answer.

Finally, if the question has multiple stages to it, e.g. question 5, part 1, part 2 and part 3, use the answers from the previous parts of the question to help you answer the latter parts. These questions often have several stages to them because they're helpfully leading you through the steps to get to a final answer in the last part of the question.

Revising Additional Maths

Follow everything as in the 'Revising Maths' section. Also, if you have the OCR Additional Maths textbook, use the 'Key Points' sections at the end of each topic, in order to help you identify the basics you need to know. It is also easier to use these, instead of the contents page, when identifying the topics you don't know how to do and the ones you need just a little more practice on. You can also use these sections to make some notes but for more detail and better explanations, refer to the full chapter.

Additional Maths exam

Follow everything as in the 'Maths Exam' section, paying particular attention to showing your workings and remembering units. This is because, in the Additional Maths exam, most of the questions are long ones, worth many marks and the units are never given for you. Unlike normal GCSE Maths, you have to write your answers on a separate 'answer sheet' – they don't always give specific places for you to write each answer and workings below each question – so make sure you clearly lay out your workings and underline your final answer, i.e. the presentation of your answer is more important.

Be aware that you may not finish the paper and that this is not the 'end of the world', especially in Additional Maths! Also, be aware that there are a lot of tedious calculations, substitutions and many stages to each answer. Therefore, it is the easiest exam in which to make 'silly mistakes' and these have worse consequences, e.g. if you make a mistake in the first stage of your workings, the rest of the workings and answer will be wrong. The most effective way to gain marks in this exam is to ensure that you have fully completed and checked your answers in 'Section A', before moving on (if you have time) to the tougher questions in 'Section B'.

Revising English

Never say "You can't revise English" – that's a common excuse for getting out of revision in this subject. Many people say this because they're used to revising factual subjects like sciences, maths etc. English is normally assessed through English Literature exams as well as separate English Language exams.

Firstly, let's look at revising English Literature. For the novels or plays that you've been studying, you need to understand, appreciate and remember the details of the key themes (or ideas) and characters of the play or novel. You need to re-read the novel or play, especially if you haven't read it for a long time. If you enjoy watching films, watch the film version of the play or novel too, if there is one.

Then, I'd recommend making your own notes, audio or visual, from revision guides for that particular novel or play. Alternatively, use class notes, book annotations or downloadable audio/video notes, of which there are quite a few for English Literature. Using an online search engine, search for '[the title of your novel/play] SmartPass guide', as well as visiting the usual 'GCSEPod' and 'BBC Bitesize' websites. This is also a subject for which the 'Friends' revision technique works well, because English is all about the opinions and ideas behind the novel or play, which often stem from discussion and deeper thinking.

For the poetry, do exactly the same. Again, you need to focus on the themes of the poem and how they're portrayed through different poetic techniques. It may be a good idea to print off a fresh copy of the poem, cut it out and stick it on to a large A3 sheet of paper so that you can annotate it with colour. Just prior to the exam, you can then use the 'Kinetic' technique as a quick reminder of the play, novel or poem.

Remember that if your exam is a closed text one, you will also have to memorise some key quotations linked to the different themes or characters of the play or novel. I'd recommend learning 2-4 quotations per major character and theme. The best way to memorise these is either by 'Look, Cover, Write, Check' for visual learners or by 'DIY Audio' (my preferred method) for audio learners.

Secondly, let's look at English Language. I find that for this subject it's most important to practise - and therefore understand - how to analyse a text, whether it's non-fiction or unseen literary prose. Then, it is important to practise writing for the different purposes, e.g. to inform, describe, explain. Therefore, I'd recommend doing past papers and paying particular attention to the mark schemes, where there is a lot to be learnt with this subject.

Make notes on what literary techniques to look out for in these texts, as well as the effects they have on the reader. Then, look at how to answer the different types of essay questions – what to include in your answer, what not to include and how your answer should be structured. These notes can be made from classwork, especially marked pieces and any marked practice papers you have. Learn what gets you those top marks by working out where marks are awarded, e.g. how many marks are awarded for correct punctuation, grammar and spelling in the essay compared to the comprehension – if a lot more are awarded for the essay, I would definitely check this before the comprehension if I was struggling for 'checking time' at the end of the exam.

Also, for both English Lang and Lit, use the mark schemes for your exam board so that you know the style in which you need to write your answer. Similarly, examiners' reports from previous exams often contain useful advice worth looking at – these can be found on your exam board's website.

English exam

Here are some important dos and don'ts for both English Language and Literature exams.

Do:

- Make a clear point

- Give evidence to back up your point, hopefully in the form of a quotation. Otherwise, give an example of an event from the text which backs up your point

- Analyse the point you've made along with the evidence. This tends to be the most difficult part but is also how the top marks are achieved. Point out any literary technique being used in the quotation and explain its use. Think about what your quotation describes, how it describes it and why – what's the significance of this quotation in relation to the point made? Think about what effect it has on the reader and therefore, why the writer has used it

- Be specific

- Mention 'the writer' or '[the writer's name]'

- Mention 'the reader'

- Use analytical words to show the examiner that you are clearly studying the text – these include: (the writer) shows, suggests, depicts, portrays, conveys, highlights, indicates, illustrates, stresses, emphasises…..(to the reader)

- Write clearly and logically, so think about and plan your answer (in your head or on paper) before you start writing

- 'Plan by Quotations', i.e. for closed book exams, plan out the structure of your essay by jotting down the fundamental quotation behind each point
- Stand out - be original in your essays

Don't:

- Narrate the story to the examiner – he already knows it very well!
- Be vague
- Generalise
- 'Feature-spot', i.e. pick out literary techniques in a text without making a point about the reason for their use
- Waste time writing excessive waffle (I hope there's none of this in this book!)

Revising Science

Whether it's Biology, Chemistry or Physics, revising science is quite straightforward. Create notes, in whatever form suits you best, from a revision guide and then go over them just before the exam, using the 'Kinetic' technique. If there are any calculations to revise, including formulae, revise these as you would do in Maths – it's all about doing practice questions (see the 'Revising Maths' section for more details).

A lot of kinetic learners enjoy, or are better at, science because they enjoy, or are better at, the practical side of the subject. If you are one of these people, it may be possible to carry out these experiments at home and this can be a very effective and enjoyable revision technique. Of course, this is only possible within reason, e.g. you could bake some fresh bread at home in order to analyse the effects of yeast in baking but you couldn't react dangerous chemicals with a Bunsen burner!

Science exam

In case any calculation questions come up in this exam, I recommend you take on board all that I've said previously in the 'Maths Exam' section. Elsewhere, it's the 'How Science Works' questions that can be a little scary, so see my previous sections about different question types ("Thinking questions" and "Misleading questions"), which are particularly important for this subject. If the exam is multiple-choice, don't be fooled into thinking it will be easy and so require little revision. Often, this means the questions are harder and the options given to you are pedantically similar, leaving you thinking it could be either of two options.

Often, this exam also requires you to read passages of text before answering questions – remember that these passages are there to help you so please read them thoroughly. Sometimes, people say "I don't bother reading those passages any more because they're just there to waste your time – they never tell you anything useful" – this is not the attitude that will deliver 100% in a GCSE.

Revising languages

Due to the fact that 50% of most language exams are aimed at testing reading and listening skills, my advice is to make sure you know as much vocabulary as possible. On your exam board's website, there is sometimes a list of all the vocabulary that could possibly feature in the exams. If not, all the vocabulary in your text book's vocabulary lists would cover this. Depending upon how confident you are with your vocabulary at the moment, the prospect of even trying to learn all these words may be very daunting.

I did give this a go but only managed to learn about 75% in the time I had. Now, I wouldn't recommend doing this unless you have lots of time, e.g. a year before the exam, or you find that most of the words on the list you know already (therefore, it's not as big a job). If you do this, I can virtually guarantee you 100% in your reading exam. If you don't choose this option, I would advise learning at least the 'General' section in the list (usually the first 4 or 5 pages). Also, your textbook or revision guide should contain a list of vocabulary at the end of each chapter – I'd definitely recommend learning at least this vocab.

Learning lots of vocabulary is the key to success but also one of the most intense, boring and time-consuming types of revision you can do. Therefore, you must take frequent breaks when doing it and always mix it up with other revision. It is more important to learn the words German to English rather than English to German, using German as an example language. This makes vocabulary learning easier and you don't have to worry about the spelling of the words. The reason I say this is that, for most of the exam, it is only necessary to be able to recognise words and translate them into English.

What about the writing and speaking exams? For the speaking exam, I would recommend learning your pre-set answers to all the possible questions, even more so if you're not very good at the subject. Use the 'DIY Audio' technique to do so – record your answers and then listen to them on the bus to school, in the car, playing footie outside… everywhere. Then, use 'Test Yourself' for practice, preferably with somebody to make it a more realistic situation. If necessary on your course, learn the presentation with 'DIY Audio' and for the role plays, practise one a night for a week or two prior to the exam. You'll only need a basic vocabulary for this exam. After having looked over some practice speaking exams, you'll know whether or not you need to learn some more basic vocabulary.

For the writing exam, as long as you have this basic vocabulary covering all the major topics, you'll be fine. Check you have this by doing practice exams. However, what is important is learning, by making visual notes, impressive constructions (e.g. idioms) and implementing them into your natural writing – they really are the key to achieving the top marks in this exam.

Here are the options for learning lots of vocabulary in your language revision:

- **'Look, Cover, Write, Check'** – good for visual learners but time-consuming

- **'Kinetic'** – good for kinetic learners and quick but not as effective in the long term

- **Association** – this is about remembering words by linking them with an image e.g. *'plancher'* makes me think of planks which can be found on the floor, hence, *'plancher'* is the French word for 'floor'. Good for creative and imaginative people, this option works best when combined with one of the two techniques above. What's more, to remember genders, you could imagine all the masculine images to be in one location and all the feminine ones in another, e.g. because *'plancher'* is masculine, I associate it with the wooden-planked floor in my house. I then imagine all other masculine words to be in my house. On the other hand, I imagine all the feminine words to be placed somewhere in my school. Sometimes, you have to make up images, e.g. if your house doesn't have a wooden floor. Otherwise, in order to overcome this problem, you could use a larger setting for your images, e.g. your whole town rather than just your house. For more information on this clever technique, see the book 'How to pass exams' by Dominic O'Brien.

- **Stare at the word** – a common but ineffective option. If you do this, stop at once – it's neither efficient nor effective.

For the listening exam, it's all about being able to recognise the words. Frequently, I'll know what a word means in English but I am unable to pick it out from the tape. Practising this skill is the only way to improve it, so buy a GCSE language CD, which either comes separately or combined with a useful revision guide – this allows you to follow the transcription of the CD in the book. Always buy the accompanying revision guide (if there is one) because otherwise, you'll never be able to look up the word that you didn't recognise. Also, when learning vocabulary, pronounce the words out loud, so that your mind registers what they sound like.

Language exams

Firstly, there is the reading exam. My first recommendation here is to read the questions before the passage so that you know what you're looking out for. Also, make sure you read everything slowly and carefully, looking out for any negative forms of the verb. Don't expect to know every word, even if you've learnt a lot of vocabulary in preparation. You won't need to know the meaning of every word to answer the questions and sometimes, you should be able to guess the meaning of a word by looking at its context within the sentence, e.g. if a sentence translates 'I ..... the beach because it's pretty', the unknown word is clearly 'like', 'love' or another similar positive word.

Then there is the listening exam, in which you must try to pull out and separate individual words from the fast stream of text that you'll hear. It's all about breaking the text down into single words which you are able to recognise. If you need to know the meaning of a certain word on the tape, in order to answer the question, but can't recognise it, do this: immediately repeat it in your head several times, so as you don't forget it. Try pronouncing it differently in order to trigger your memory. If this fails, write the word down in all the different ways in which you think it could be spelt. If this fails, give up and move on quickly, only returning to it if you have spare time.

Before the tape begins, spend your reading time wisely so as you know what to listen out for in the tape. If there are any multiple-choice questions, think about which words you would be likely to hear if the answer was option 1, 2 or 3. For example, the question asking 'Where did Sarah go?' might have the option 'London' as a possible answer. Think about how else this could be phrased on the tape, e.g. 'Sarah visited the capital of England'. If you don't have a clue what the answer is, write down the common sense answer, e.g. Sarah went to …… to find her lost bag – here the common sense answer could be 'lost property'.

Next, there's the speaking exam. Don't be scared to ask for the question to be repeated and learn how to say this in the relevant language beforehand, e.g. '*Répétez-vous, s'il-vous-plaît* '. If you need some thinking time, just say, "Mmm… good question" in the relevant language. Similarly, feel free to pause for a couple of seconds before answering each question, even if you've learnt the answer off by heart. This will help you avoid making 'silly mistakes', which are so easily done under pressure. If somebody asked you what you liked about your school in English, you'd have to think about the answer before speaking - it sounds much more natural than charging straight in with a pre-learnt answer.

Speak clearly and don't be shocked if a question you haven't prepared for crops up or your teacher slightly re-words a question to suit the situation – just use the ideas from your pre-set answers to come up with a new answer. If you need to say a particular word but don't have a clue what it is in that language, describe it in different terms or look for a synonym, e.g. if you didn't know the word for 'coat', you could say a 'jacket' or, for a 'laptop', you could say a 'small computer'. Whatever you do, always speak in the relevant language – never speak any English as this is not impressive or the purpose of the exam.

Finally, there's the writing exam (if you have one). Firstly, don't write a lot more than the word limit because you'll get no credit for doing so. Therefore, it is a waste of valuable checking time and is likely to increase the number of mistakes you make. Also, think before you write, because you need to make sure you include everything (tenses, constructions, content) within the word limit. Finally, check your essays at the end of the exam for all those 'silly mistakes'.

However, the most important point to make about this exam is that YOU control how difficult you make it. Obviously, you want to make it as easy as possible for yourself. Therefore, choose wisely what you write about and the words you use. If given a choice, or a vague title of the essay, write about the topic for which you have the most vocabulary and personal ideas. Choose the exact words you use wisely, e.g. if you're unsure of the spelling of 'sometimes', use a similar word, e.g. 'usually', 'rarely', 'occasionally' or 'often' instead. Even consider leaving this word out completely, even if what you say is not strictly true.

In some GCSE language courses nowadays, you are allowed to use a dictionary in the writing exam. If you are, don't rely on this to write your answer – you simply wouldn't have enough time to write a long enough answer and a dictionary wouldn't tell you, for example, what ending a verb would need to have. Do use the dictionary though if you need to check the spelling of a word or want to include some more complicated vocabulary in your answer.

Take advantage of the freedom of choice that you're given in these writing exams, while still ensuring you write about everything you're asked to. Don't write what you'd write if the essay was in English, which would often include words and sentences you don't know how to form in this other language. Write using the German you know, not trying to use the German you don't know (using German, my favourite language, as an example again!).

Revising History

Firstly, this is a subject in which it is important to gather as much knowledge and impressive facts as you can. Make detailed notes, in whichever form you wish, on the different topics. Then, you must practise and learn how to answer your exam board's particular style of questions. Every time you learn something new about the way in which you should answer the different questions, write it down so that you can review this before the GCSE exam. Also, read some of the mark schemes and exam reports for more advice on specific exam technique for History.

History exam

In the exam, extensive knowledge is not only required in order to fully explain historical events in the essays, but also to maximise your chances of immediately understanding sources. In fact, the mark schemes of source questions often specify that a candidate must show direct use of their own knowledge in their answer, in order to achieve the top mark band. It also helps you with the speed of recognising the correct meaning behind a source, something which is important for this tightly timed exam. What's more, there are different degrees to which you can read into these sources and, with more knowledge you're more likely to spot the significance of deeper, hidden details.

For this exam, there is a definite way in which each question should be answered. Remember to 'tick all the boxes', e.g. an answer to a question about the reliability of a source must mention its date, author, content's honesty, purpose, format, etc. and a question which starts off 'Which source do you trust more…' is asking for an answer which deals with both sources, their reliability and a conclusion.

For any essay questions, write clearly and logically, so think about and plan your answer (in your head or on paper) before you start writing. Use paragraphs and show how you've identified a point, described and explained it, making sure you refer back to the original question. In order to successfully and fully explain things in this exam, it is important to state obvious points. Don't expect to have the time to check all your answers and don't worry about spelling and grammar checking if the mark scheme doesn't award marks for this. Also, as with all essays, don't waste time writing excessive waffle!

Revising ICT

As well as making notes on the relevant topics, this is a subject where completing, marking and learning from past papers is important. All sorts of questions tend to crop up – some that don't seem to be linked to the topics on the syllabus or could easily be wrongly interpreted. You must learn how to interpret certain questions and revise any extra topics you find in the mark schemes which you didn't already know about.

ICT exam

Sometimes, this exam is very factual, asking for advantages, disadvantages, uses, explanations and definitions, which you'll find very easy if you've revised properly. However, the exam can also include "misleading questions" (see the earlier section for more details) – unfortunately, it is hard to predict the balance between factual and "misleading questions" on the ICT paper.

Remember not to miss out on extra marks by writing a conclusion for any 'Discuss' questions, i.e. where you give the pros and cons of a subject. There are mark schemes which award a bonus mark for a conclusion. It is also important to state seemingly obvious points in order to fully explain topics in this exam. Some mark schemes, on a six mark question, award three marks for three points and the remaining three marks can only be gained via full explanations of all three points – these could easily be forgotten as the explanations seem to be common sense.

If you are taking a practical ICT exam, as well as a theory paper, take into account these few tips. Firstly, make sure you keep track of time because it's important to ensure that you complete the whole exam - but without unnecessarily rushing. I would recommend scanning through the whole paper at the start of the exam so that you know exactly what's coming – this will also allow you to easily estimate how long you should spend on each question. Additionally, if you get stuck on part of a question, do not hesitate to use the help system incorporated in the software you are using (only if you are allowed to!) – if this doesn't work, leave the question out and come back to it at the end if you have enough time.

Summary

The five most important tips from this chapter are:

- **Answer how the examiners want you to**, not how YOU want to

- Answer **logically**, specifically and clearly

- Use **language CDs** for listening and oral practice

- Don't be afraid of **stating the obvious**

- Revise each subject using the style that **suits it best**

If you follow this advice, you will be well on your way to achieving 100% in a GCSE!

Round-Up Time

We are now coming towards the end of this book – phew (both for me writing it and you reading it no doubt!). I hope you've got something out of this book. Life is all about learning and, with this book, I hope you've learnt something which will ultimately result in you performing at your highest potential in each and every GCSE you take. Throughout the book, I hope I've increased your motivation and encouraged you to achieve. Before we round-up 'How to achieve 100% in a GCSE', here are the factual reasons for wanting to achieve top GCSE results.

Why bother with GCSEs?

Firstly, GCSEs are vital as they give you choice in the job market - which is becoming increasingly competitive - resulting in you getting the job you want.

In addition, GCSEs give you choice in the increasingly competitive further education market – college and university admissions do look at your GCSE results, which are often the deciding factor between candidates.

Finally, the most important reason for doing GCSEs is for a sense of personal achievement because without this the two practical reasons above are invalid.

A parent once said to me, "What does it matter if [her son] gets an A or an A* in Physics? He'll still get into his sixth form college." Similarly, a friend once said to me "What's the point in aiming for 100% in a GCSE when this won't appear on your university application?" What is in common with both questions? An opinion of GCSEs that is very restrictive, simply practical and doesn't take into account that this is an opportunity to fulfill your potential. It is like someone saying to David Beckham at the age of twelve, "Why keep practising that free kick, when you're already the best player in the school team?"

I emphasise the word 'personal' because GCSE success won't happen if you're only doing it for your Mum, Dad, teacher or anybody else, nagging at you to revise. In order to be successful, you have to want to do it for yourself. Many people ask me if my parents forced me to revise – the answer is not at all. If I had wanted, I could have got away with doing very little revision. However, this is why most of my motivation comes from myself (self-motivation). This is more effective than if the motivation is coming from others because it is YOU (not them) doing the revision and exams.

I emphasise the word 'achievement' because this is your reward for preparing hard for your exams – a sense of achievement and satisfaction, something to be proud of, being able to tell others the good news, being complimented by them and feeling happy knowing you've done your best. If you are somebody who hasn't worked hard for a long time and who a lot of people have 'written off', this could be the time to 'pull out all the stops'. Wouldn't it be amazing to surprise your parents and teachers with your GCSE results? This could be the time to 'turn over a new leaf' and prove wrong everyone who has ever discredited you.

Rob's formula

What makes up a GCSE?

To have any chance of gaining 100% in a GCSE, we need to think about exactly what a GCSE consists of. This then creates a unique formula, in which all areas need to be completed successfully in order to secure those top marks. Here is my formula for achieving 100% in a GCSE:

$$C + L + R + E = 100\%$$

You need to get each part of this formula spot on to achieve that dream result.

Can you guess what any of the letters stand for?

C = Controlled Assessment

Controlled assessment replaces the old-style 'Coursework' in a lot of GCSE syllabuses nowadays. It is essentially coursework that is done within a restricted time period in class in exam conditions. You will however have had time to prepare your answer prior to the assessment and you can often take brief notes in with you. Controlled assessments will always be marked by your teacher, before being moderated externally by the exam board. But don't worry – it is unusual for controlled assessment marks to be changed drastically during the moderation process.

Often, students find it easier to score higher marks in controlled assessments than in exams, primarily because there are less restrictions and less pressure. You should take advantage of the controlled assessments you do – don't dismiss them because they don't feel very important at the time. You will live to regret it if you miss an A* by one mark, which you could have easily got by preparing ten minutes more for your controlled assessment. Nearer to the time of the exam, it will be very helpful to you. Having gathered lots of marks in advance, you will be able to feel more confident, which should reduce any nerves you have.

L = Lesson Time

Don't waste it! Concentrate in lessons and you'll have less revision to do at the end. Ask if you don't understand something while the teacher can still explain it to you – otherwise, you will have to figure it out for yourself when the exams come round. Make use of every second of every lesson from day one to the end. If you finish copying down notes before the others, try and begin memorising the information (rather than throwing pencils across the classroom!). Appreciate others who are trying to learn – help them, don't distract them. This will all help reduce the amount of time you'll have to revise when the exams arrive, although I see how difficult it is to think of the exams when they seem so far away.

If you don't listen, focus and get involved during lessons, you're going to find it very difficult to revise because you'll be learning the material almost from scratch. This means more revision, difficult revision and lots of having to understand information – not a pleasant combination.

R = Revision

We've talked a lot about this! I can't stress how important it is to ensure your revision is 'quality, not quantity'. Without efficient and effective revision, achieving top results in the exams is impossible and, therefore, this is a vital part of the formula to ensure all that lesson time hasn't gone to waste.

E = Exam Technique

This may include very simple points, of which all are in the relevant chapter of this book, but it is crucial to ensure that all the revision you've done doesn't go to waste in the exam. Exam pressure can do all sorts of things to you, so knowing exam technique beforehand is an important part of the winning GCSE formula to ensure you don't carelessly throw marks away.

And finally…

Good luck with your exams and thank you for reading this book. Remember, two years worth of hard work is being tested by a two hour exam, so make sure you do yourself justice, prepare for your exams and achieve your potential in your GCSEs......... Time for me to have a rest now – oh dear, it's the end of my summer holidays!

If you have any thoughts, comments or questions from reading the book, please do not hesitate to contact me through the book's website. It's great to hear from you!

www.howtoachieve.webs.com

If you have found this book useful, please submit a review at -

www.amazon.co.uk

Printed in Great Britain
by Amazon.co.uk, Ltd.,
Marston Gate.